CURRA to

SANTIAGO

MY CAMINO

A pilgrim's journey to the Shrine
of St James

JAMES KEOGHAN

Copyright

Dedication

Dedicated to the memory of
Captain Ristéard Mac Eochagáin
and his son Brian

The Author

James Keoghan was born in 1944 in Cork City. On leaving school he began an apprenticeship as a stone mason. However, by 1960 the call of the sea could no longer be ignored. He signed on as a deck boy on board the ship, The Irish Hazel on a voyage to New Orleans. In the following years at sea he would undertake many voyages, taking him to a great variety of ports around the world, big and small, exotic and mundane. In 1966 he was awarded a testimonial by the Royal Humane Society for the saving of life at sea. After steady promotion in his career he attained the position of First Officer on some of the most modern tankers of the day. He finally came ashore in the late seventies. He now works in the architectural profession. James is the father of three grown up children and lives in Kinsale, County Cork. His love of the sea and interest in Spain continue to inspire him.

Acknowledgements

In writing this book I sought, and was freely given advice by many people; fellow pilgrims, friends of long standing and in some cases even complete strangers. I am deeply grateful to all of them.

I am especially indebted to the following as without their assistance this work would not have been completed. My son in-law Rory Hanly who first suggested I write this book, and for his continued encouragement throughout the process. The old sailor and author John Young for his initial edit of the manuscript. Neanon Gullery, a wonderful linguist for her expert help with my Spanish translations and Paul O'Reilly for his advice on the cover design. My brother Gerard Keoghan for his historical research into the role played by our ancestors in the events surrounding the Battle of Kinsale and its aftermath. My late cousin Breen Keoghan, master fly fisherman, expert shot and historian, who instilled in me the determination to undertake the adventure. He never wavered in his belief that this book would be published but sadly did not live to read it. My deep appreciation to my friend and mentor Paul Whelan for his advice, guidance, and especially his attention to detail in correcting the many drafts I burdened him with.

To my wife Teresa for her encouragement during the times when I doubted that I would ever reach Santiago and for her practical support and guidance. This is my way of saying thank you for being so patient.

I am deeply indebted to Orla Kelly and the team at Orla Kelly Publishing, for the indispensable help and guidance that turned publishing this book from a fraught and stressful experience into a very enjoyable journey for me.

As for the people referred to at the beginning, there are far too many to thank individually here.

However, I sought advice only from people who I believe to be clever and whom I admire. Of course they know who they are. My sincere thanks.

James Keoghan

Contents

Preface

It is said that a pilgrim is a believer who undertakes a journey to a holy place to ask for a pardon, to beg a favour, or to give thanks for a blessing received. Santiago de Compostela in Galicia in the northwest corner of Spain is such a place, a place where tradition has it that the relics of the apostle James reside.

A pilgrimage to Compostela, '*The field of stars*', located at the very edge of the known world in ancient times, has the power to change lives forever for the modern pilgrim as much as it did for his medieval counterpart.

Since the early middle ages many thousands of pilgrims from all over Europe have made their way on foot to the city of Santiago de Compostela, to worship at the shrine of St James.

Along the way they could expect to face robbery, danger, hardship, sickness and even death at the hands of the bandits and brigands that lay in wait for them on the road.

For the ancient pilgrim who reached Santiago the return journey was no less dangerous and many were never to see their homes again.

In more recent times, especially since the 1960s when backpacking and trekking became popular, this ancient pilgrim route underwent somewhat of a revival as it became more accessible for people from all over the world.

Although the dangers faced along the way by the ancient pilgrims are no more, various hardships still remain for the modern pilgrim to contend with as he or she tramps along day after day, over high windswept mountains, through endless open spaces with little or no shade, suffering blisters, backache, ligament problems, heat stroke and stomach upsets, not to mention bed bugs and sleep deprivation due to the choruses of chronic snoring that can frequently be encountered in dormitories of up to sixty or more bunks in some *albergues* (hostels) along the way.

While the reason for undertaking this walk may no longer be predominately religious, of course for some it still is, though I suspect for a small minority. For many who attempt it these days it can still be a spiritual experience, while others may be inspired by the deep history and traditions of it all.

More are seeking answers, trying to understand some occurrence in their life, such as a breakdown in a relationship or a bereavement.

More still are simply taking stock of their lives, maybe trying to work out why some things are the way they are, undertaking this medieval odyssey in the hope they will acquire some beneficial insights or answers that will allow them to get on with their lives.

Whatever people's reasons are for undertaking this pilgrimage, and there are as many reasons as there are pilgrims walking the camino, I feel certain that the vast majority would admit to encountering a strange, yet tangible feeling of connection to all who have gone before them, a feeling of belonging – like a small pebble in this great river of humanity that has been flowing, west across northern Spain to Santiago, uninterrupted since the middle ages.

All along the way are medieval crosses with

arrows marking the way to Santiago. At the base of these crosses one sees mounds of small stones. It is an age old custom of the camino that the passing pilgrim picks up one of these stones and carries it along to the next cross he reaches.

With that simple act the pilgrim recreates the link in the unbroken chain of pilgrims, ancient and modern.

The majority of modern day pilgrims setting out to walk to the shrine of St James will begin their journey in the medieval village of St-Jean-Pied-de-Port on the French side of the Pyrenees.

By so doing, they follow in the footprints of the many hundreds of thousands of pilgrims who have, for over a thousand years, sought to undertake this ancient pilgrimage across the north of Spain to the cathedral in Santiago de Compostela.

Like the ancient pilgrim, not all of these modern day pilgrims would complete the journey.

This route is known as the *Camino Francés* (French Way) or just, the *Camino* (the way).

At the start, the *Camino Francés* transverses the Basque country ascending the Pyrenees, those wild and majestic mountains separating France and Spain. It then descends into Lower Navarra on the Spanish side.

From there it winds its way west through the provinces of Navarra and La Rioja before crossing into the autonomous region of Castilla y León and its provinces of Burgos, Palencia and finally into Galicia, where it finishes in the magnificent Praza do Obradoiro in the great city of Santiago de Compostela.

CHAPTER ONE
My Camino

Early on the 23rd of May 2014 I set out from my home at Currahoo, a small shallow creek on the southern bank of the river Bandon, a short distance upriver from the old historical town of Kinsale and its famous harbour, located on the south coast of Ireland.

The river at this point is quite wide with lovely views of the opposite bank with its gentle, rolling green fertile fields, interspersed here and there with small stands of woodland. The townland of Tissaxon Beg at the foot of Ardmartin Hill can be seen further to the north in the distance.

It is there that the Battle of Kinsale took place on Christmas Eve 1601. It was an event that would resonate strongly with my desire to undertake this ancient pilgrimage to Santiago de Compostela to honour my ancestors who fought at that battle all those years ago.

After taking an early morning train to Dublin, I caught a flight to Biarritz in France and a bus transfer to the rail station in Bayonne.

There I joined a diverse group of pilgrims, taking the old bus up to the quaint medieval Basque village of St-Jean-Pied-de-Port high in the Pyrenees, arriving there late that evening.

St-Jean-Pied-de-Port was to be the starting

point of my camino. I intended to walk the eight hundred kilometres from here to Santiago de Compostela. I hoped to complete the distance in around forty-three days, staying in the *Albergues de Peregrinos* (pilgrim hostels) that are to be found in the towns and villages all along the way.

I also planned to meet up with my two daughters and their friend, who intended to walk the final one hundred kilometres from the town of Sarria to the end of the journey in Compostela with me.

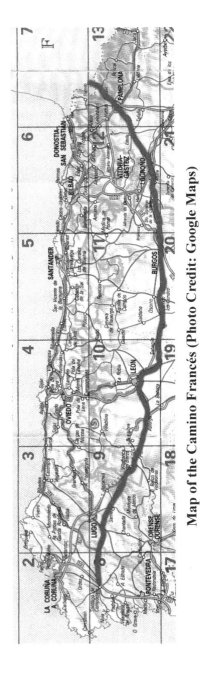

Map of the Camino Francés (Photo Credit: Google Maps)

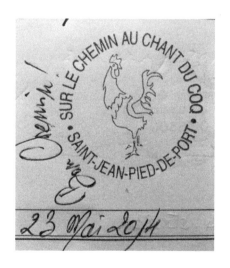

CHAPTER TWO
Crossing the Pyrenees

At first light the next morning, after presenting myself at the Pilgrim Office and receiving my first *sello* (stamp) in my *Credencial del Peregrino* (pilgrim passport), I lifted my pack onto my back.

I walked down the old cobbled Rue Centrale, passed through the famous Porte d'Espagne, the ancient gateway to Spain, and crossed the bridge over the river Nive, thereby taking my first step on the camino.

Almost immediately after leaving the village of Saint-Jean-Pied-de-Port behind, the pilgrims come to an intersection in the road.

This is where the first of the red and white signs that mark the camino on the French side of the Pyrenees appear and it is at this point also that the decision must be made whether to continue on the road along the valley through Valcarlos, or take the strenuous uphill climb over the Col de Lepoeder, known as the Route de Napoleon.

I chose the latter, and with that decision made the climb up the mountain suddenly begin in earnest and the effect on the senses both immediate and sobering.

All the preparation and planning in the months leading up to my departure, the studying of the guide books, the agonizing over what items to pack and even the selection of the backpack itself, making sure that it is the right size and weight for

Port d'Espagne-First step on the journey to Santiago

me. Had I thought of everything? Was I ready for this adventure? Would I make it to Santiago?

All of those questions were swirling through my mind at that moment as I started up this very steep hill, constantly adjusting the straps of my backpack, trying to make it more comfortable.

The anxiety of venturing alone into the unknown, coupled with the fear of failure, unexpectedly made me feel morbid.

Despite this state of affairs, I told myself that this was a big test at the very beginning of the camino and would demand not only stamina, but all the reserves of mental strength I could muster to getting up and over the Pyrenees; safety must be my priority for now.

By mid-morning, the sun had broken through the cloud cover and the morning's slight chill began to disappear. Before long my own cloud had lifted somewhat and I began to take notice of and appreciate my surroundings.

As I climbed higher the roadside verge was thick with yellow and white alpine poppies. There was no traffic on the road as I walked upward through this hilly but pleasant green countryside with its scattering of small Basque working farms.

Just after midday I overtook a group of three

elderly female pilgrims from Holland. They seemed to be walking very slowly. They were the only ones I had met since I started. I answered their greeting with "*Buen camino*", the traditional greeting of the camino, and after exchanging a few pleasantries I moved on.

I was now feeling the effects of all this exertion. The day had become hot but the air was clean and clear, and after another hour's walking I decided to take a break by the roadside. After a very pleasant, if simple, lunch of bread and cheese I sat there for a short while, propped against my backpack.

I took in the magnificent views back down the valley, far below and beyond to the various villages and hamlets that dot the French side of the Pyrenees. Soon it was time to get moving again, so I got to my feet, cleared my lungs, adjusted my pack, and restarted the climb.

With food inside me I was now in good spirits, if

slowing somewhat from the mornings pace. Mid-afternoon having come around a sharp bend in the road, the refuge at Orrison suddenly appeared among the tall pines a short distance ahead. Within minutes I was standing in the reception area and booking in for the night.

After showering and changing out of my now sweat-soaked walking gear and tending to the first of the many blisters I was to acquire along the way, I donned, for the first time, what I came to call my 'going ashore dress uniform'.

This consisted of my only pair of light slacks, the least creased of my two shirts and the piece de resistance of the whole affair, a paisley patterned cravat, no less. This was to become my trademark on the walk, and proved a psychological lift for me later on in the walk when the going started to get tough.

Although many pilgrims never changed out of their walking clothes at all or merely changed to a spare set when relaxing around the *albergue* after their day's trek or going out for a meal in the evenings.

No matter how shattered I felt at the end of a long days walk, the ensemble was carefully extracted from where it resided in its protective plastic turkey bag at the bottom of my back pack.

Then even more carefully folded and placed under my pillow for the duration of a siesta, that I took to having each day on reaching my destination. Thereby getting a kind of rudimentary pressing before I ventured down to *la cena* (dinner) or going out socialising in the evening.

To say the results were more often than not, less than satisfactory would be an understatement. 'But doesn't the lord love a trier anyhow?'

So after my siesta I went down to the bar where a few pilgrims had gathered having a drink before *la cena*, of course all of those there were strangers to me. I wasn't to know then that before long some were destined to become my walking companions and good friends.

But for now, sitting there listening to those pilgrims discussing the day's hard climb up to here and what may lie ahead tomorrow. I was feeling somewhat pleased with myself that I had completed the first day of my camino, a steep climb of around eight hundred metres.

Somewhat philosophically it dawned on me that I had become the newest link in that thousand-year pilgrim chain.

It is the tradition of the *albergue* at Orrison, the first of the many I would stay in along the camino, that after *la cena* every pilgrim is asked to stand up and announce where he or she came from, their reason for doing the camino, and how far they hoped to walk.

When it came to my turn, I simply informed my fellow pilgrims that I came from near the small town of Kinsale on the south coast of Ireland, that my reason for doing the camino was to honour the memory of my ancestors, but that right now, I was not quite sure what I was doing here among complete strangers in this *albergue* that seemed to be clinging precariously to the side of a mountain.

I also said that I hoped to complete the whole journey to Santiago and if, for whatever reason I did not complete my pilgrimage, I would not be returning to try another time.

Along the way I was to learn many lessons for making camino life a little more agreeable. Some of those lessons took more time than others to sink in, but after spending a restless first night on the trail perched high up in a rather rickety top bunk in this *albergue*, I determined that come what may, whatever it took – beg, cajole or grovel – the much prized and sought after bottom bunk would be my nocturnal habitat for the duration of this adventure.

Of the thirty-two pilgrims there that night,

twenty-four said that like me they also hoped to complete the pilgrimage, the rest planned to walk sections of the route. In the end only eight of the pilgrims there that night actually completed the whole journey to Santiago de Compostela.

The next morning, in poor visibility and with continuous light rain and mist, I continued the climb up this narrow, winding, mountain road, overtaking and being overtaken by other pilgrims along the way, always with the salutation of 'buen camino'. The landscape changed as I climbed higher.

In contrast to the previous day's pleasant green rolling slopes of the Basque countryside with its pastures and woodland, it changed to a bleak and desolate mountain moorland that is home to the pyrenean wild horse and black-faced sheep.

Overhead a variety of birds of prey including kite, sparrow hawk, falcon and the magnificent griffon vultures soared high over the landscape.

Landscape of the Pyrenees (Photo credit: Ajiemar)

I came to Cruceiro by late morning, a wayside cross and memorial. It appeared suddenly out of the mist with a group of pilgrims milling around it and all looking quite grim. The route leaves the road here and continues on a rough grass track that climbs over the Col de Bentarte ridge.

Once over this ridge, I attached myself to a group of about ten people, all walking in single file for safety. As conditions worsened, it became increasingly difficult to make out even the walker just immediately ahead. There wasn't much talk.

I felt some were suffering. After only a brief rest the group moved on again. Everyone just wanted to keep going and get off the summit.

Visibility was down to a few feet, then word came down the line for everyone to close up, not to lose sight of the walker in front and to call out if that happened.

We were now walking almost on top of each other. It became a real struggle that seemed to go on forever. After what seemed like an eternity, at around noon, the highest point of the climb was behind us.

This had been a difficult steep climb over the rocks and through the gap at Col de Lepoeder. No one lingered. There was nothing to see. After a very short time the ground had a definite downward slope. We were through the pass and were descending.

In these conditions it was easy to see how some pilgrims could get lost up here, and how some came to grief attempting this Route de Napoleon rather than the lower road through Valcarlos.

Indeed, I was to later meet a brother and sister from Los Angeles who had been unable to get a bed in the *albergue* at Orrison the night before. They had no option but to continue in deteriorating and dangerous conditions until they were almost done in. They were fortunate to find an emergency hut located just below the pass. Here they spent a cold and frightening night. They were later to become two of my closest camino friends.

In this thick fog, the descent from the Col de Lepoeder at fourteen hundred meters was brutal. The group I had been walking with had now strung out, some moving ahead and out of sight, while others lagged behind, descending slowly.

**Descent from the Col de Lepoeder in fog
(Photo credit: Ajiemar)**

After a while I overtook two Spanish middle aged ladies. I greet them with *"Hola, que tal?"* (hello, how's it going), and got a reply of *"bien, mas o menos"* (okay, more or less). It turned out they were sisters, one a nun.

On their third camino, they admitted this was the worst weather they had encountered on the Pyrenees. They confessed they were quite fatigued by it all and were considering giving up when they reached Roncesvalles.

We chatted some more for a while, shared some biscuits and then with a "buen camino", I bid them farewell and moved on down the path. I felt sad that their dream of getting to Santiago for the third time may have come to an end. I was never to see them again.

I continued to descend down through deep wooded ravines with the ground soft and wet underfoot and a leafy canopy overhead. I then came to a stone border marker confirming I had crossed into Spain.

Further down the track, I crossed a tarmac road and entered an enormous beech wood, reputed to be one of the largest remaining in Europe. Here the ground was firmer and the walking became easier, but it seemed to go on forever with no sign of the end of the descent through the trees.

Then finally, after what seemed like an eternity

I came to a clearing at the side of a small river leading to a gravel path and there it was.

Suddenly before me was the great Augustinian monastery of Roncesvalles and a bed for the night. It was 7pm in the evening. I was wet, I had painful blisters and had also developed a ligament problem in my left leg from the continuous pressure on my knees that shocked my whole body with every step on the steep descent down the mountain.

This condition would make walking very painful during the next week for me. In a few minutes I was at the great wall of the monastery and entered through an arch leading to the square where the reception area is located.

At last I was able to drop my *mochila* (back pack) on the stone floor and proceeded to have my *Credencial del Peregrino* stamped with the grand medieval *sello* of Roncesvalles.

Then after paying for my bed for the night I

was directed to a dormitory by two very kind *hospitaleros* (volunteer attendants) and collapsed in a heap on a vacant bunk, not any bunk, but one of the prized bottom bunks no less. With that, for me, one of the lessons for surviving the camino had been learned.

Roncesvalles (Valley of thorns) is the major gateway for Spanish pilgrims coming up from the south to join the *Camino Francés* (the French way). Everything here is steeped in history, from the mausoleum housing the tomb of Sancho VII and his wife Clemencia to the Silo de Carlomagno, the reputed burial place of the slaughtered rear guard of Charlemagne's army.

The medieval atmosphere here is palatable. Augustinian monks in the monastery have, since the twelfth century, been tending to all pilgrims that pass this way: healthy and sick, Christian, Jew, pagan, heretic and vagabond. All were and still are welcome. Although tired, I felt a sense of achievement in having made it across the Pyrenees. So off I went after *la cena* to the nightly pilgrim mass in the *Real Collegiata de Santa Maria* (The Royal Collegiate Church of Saint Mary).

The mass with its special blessing for pilgrims of all faiths was concelebrated in Spanish by four elderly priests. Sadly, they were all that remained of the once large congregation of over a hundred monks.

At the end of the mass came the medieval blessing. It was a very poignant moment. I believe the congregation present that night, consisting of pilgrims and a few locals, had to have been touched by it. I know I certainly was.

As we filed out into the darkness I noticed more than one damp cheek. This was to be the first of many great churches and monasteries I would enter as I progressed along the way.

Date: 24 . 05 . 2014

CHAPTER THREE

Walking Through History in Navarra

The weather stayed wet and very cold all through Navarra, a fiercely independent mountainous region with a turbulent past, that includes the massacre of the rear guard of Charlemagne's army by the Basques at Roncesvalles in around 778 AD as revenge for the destruction of Pamplona despite assurance that the city would not be harmed.

In more modern times this region has attracted many foreign writers: notably Ernest Hemmingway who stayed for extended periods in Pamplona and Burguete writing of the regions customs and way of life and, of course, the classic novel '*The Sun Also Rises*'.

The famous running of the bulls during the week-long festival of San Fermin held in Pamplona in July is the highlight of the year in these parts. Hundreds of people, mostly young men, take their lives in their hands by running in front of the bulls through the streets of the old-quarter to the bull ring.

The next morning, I was one of the last to leave the monastery and it was still only 8am. On rising I had spent some time rearranging where everything was to be stored in my *mochila* for the trek ahead with the consequent delay.

It was raining lightly and the world looked quite grim as I set off, taking a path through a rather boggy beech wood alongside the road and my mood was not improved as I passed a large sign declaring, 'To Santiago, 790 Km'.

Further on, *the way*, as it's known, traversed through the old town of Burguete, then continued mostly through more beech woods and along rough paths that climbed over steep hills as it made its way between the small villages of Espinal and Puente de la Rabia.

There according to legend, any animal led three times around the centre arch of its medieval bridge would be cured of rabies. Along this section the camino also crosses over the river Arga many times until finally leaving it at Punto La Reina.

Late in the afternoon on reaching the top of what was to be the last climb of the day, I was very relieved to see the old medieval bridge leading to the entrance to the town Zubiri. This was my destination for to-day. It had been a long, tough day of walking, not helped by this ligament problem which seemed to be getting worse, by comparison making my blisters almost feel like old friends.

Arriving at the *Albergue Zaldiko* in Zubiri I was greeted by Desiree and Natasha, two barmaids from Alberta in Canada I had met that first night in the *albergue* at Orrison.

They were always great fun, never taking anything too seriously. They would leave the *albergue* very early each morning, but stop at almost every village along the way, where they could be found under the ubiquitous sun umbrella outside some bar or other forcing down a *cerveza fría* (cold beer) or two, while watching the world of the camino go by. However, for all that, they made it to Santiago on the same day I did.

Later that evening I was also to meet some more old friends from that first night at Orrison.

Among them were Graham and Antoinette, walking companions, he from Dublin and she from Carlow (Ireland).

Graham was an old-hand having already done a previous camino. He was a tall and lean guy in his mid-forties, a very intense energetic individual and a fast walker always helping people, whether it was giving medical advice, usually on the subject of treating blisters, or keeping beds for the laggards like myself in the hostels.

**Walking companions, Graham from Dublin and
Antoinette from Carlow (Ireland)**

In real life he was a residential social care worker with the Father McVerry trust, a charity in Dublin dedicated to the homeless. He became known to everyone as *El Comandante* (The Commander). Graham was the first of all the pilgrims I met along the way to reach Compostela.

On the other hand, Antoinette was a small, slight, very friendly and caring young woman in her early thirties. Back in Carlow she was a Corporal in the Reserve Defence Forces having served for eleven years and was going home from Burgos to take up a new job in the social services. She was also very fit and never complained, no matter how hard the going was.

Our conversations always seemed to revolve around the subject of romance and the difficulty of meeting someone nice and caring that might lead to a meaningful relationship, and on that subject I dispensed liberal quantities of some very questionable advice as we tramped along together.

Also in the group was Eoin, a music student from Dublin in his twenties, whom I christened '*Ho Chi Minh*' as he was developing a rather scraggly goatee beard. He too was a good walker and unusually, he never seemed to suffer from blisters.

Eoin was another one of the group to walk all the way to Santiago. Incredibly, shortly after my return to Kinsale as I was entering the local supermarket I ran into him. It turned out he was passing through on vacation with his family, a small world indeed.

It was also in Zubiri that I met Marie, an independent, gentle and very stylish lady I would put in her early sixties. She was walking alone. Originally from Northern Ireland, she had recently retired from a long career nursing with the McMillan palliative care trust in Surrey in England, where she continues to live.

On seeing how I was limping painfully, she took me aside and advised me to wear an elastic bandage on my injured knee while walking, and prescribed a lotion to be applied liberally and without fail before setting out every morning, during my midday stop and again when I got off the trail each evening.

Tom, Roly, Sara, Desiree, Natasha, Antoinette, Graham, Marie and the author with unnamed Americans

Even now I remember her words clearly. "James," she said somewhat sternly, "your self-diagnosed ligament problem is really a spasm and it will clear in a week or so – provided you follow my advice." True to her word that is what happened, for in a few days I was feeling much better and walking normally.

Marie was only accompanying us as far as Pamplona but was always lovely to chat and joke with as we walked along.

I recall one occasion I rather flippantly said to her, "Marie, so what is one of those black protestants from the North (of Ireland) doing walking this camino, anyway?" She stopped, turned to me and quietly said, "Actually I was brought up a Methodist in Portadown. My father was a minister in the church there, but I converted to Catholicism when I took up nursing." "May God forgive you", I responded and we both burst out laughing.

To me she came across as most kind, an understanding and considerate person, and it was an honour to have walked some of the way with her.

I reached Pamplona, the first city the camino passes through after four days of walking. Pamplona, is a vibrant university city founded by the Roman General Pompaelo in the first century B.C. Through its long and dramatic history, it has been closely linked with pilgrims, some of whom in earlier times ventured no further and settled in the city.

Here I was lucky to get the last bed for the night in the German hostel. That evening after dinner I made my way to Hemingway's old haunt, the famous Café Irima, located on the Plaza Del Castillo within the old town walls.

Sitting there sipping a beer with some of my travelling companions and looking out on this beautiful square lined with large plane trees in the fading evening light, the enormity of what I had committed myself to in attempting this pilgrimage was beginning to dawn on me.

Most of my fellow pilgrims decided to take the next day off to rest up, but I elected to continue on and left early in the morning, alone and in a slight drizzle.

Leaving Pamplona's old town behind I followed the *flechas amarillas* (the yellow arrows) marking the route through the Citadel park by way of a surfaced walk called the Vuelta del Castillo, continuing past the gardens of the university to the medieval bridge over the river Sadar.

Once over the river I crossed a rather busy road and took the path opposite until I came to a steel bridge over a railway line and then uphill to the small town of Cizur Menor. There I took refuge from the rain in a bar and had my first *café con leche* (white coffee) of the day. Refreshed I took off again taking a broad, fairly level clay track running between corn fields.

Further on the track climbs steeply and breaks out on to a country road leading up into the village of Zariquiegui with its small but charming church of *San Miguel* (Saint Michael) built in the Gothic style.

Apart from the church there is just a scattering of village dwellings, with one of them converted into a small *albergue* with a nice cosy bar and restaurant.

Although it was only early afternoon I was feeling tired and to tell the truth, a little lonely as I had encountered very few other pilgrims all morning. So I decided to call a halt for the day here and booked in to the *albergue*.

I was the first pilgrim to arrive that day and I was glad I did so, as it turned out, because as other pilgrims arrived later in the afternoon the talk was all about the fearsome *Alto del Perdón* (hill of forgiveness), seven hundred and ninety metres high and made famous in the movie 'The Way' staring the American actor Martin Sheehan, that was lurking just ahead.

When I turned in that night it was with some relief that I had not walked on, and would be fresh tackling its ascent in the morning.

I may have been the first pilgrim to arrive in the village that day, but the next morning I was the last to leave. The weather had changed for the better and the morning was bright with a clear blue sky and little wind. This put me in good spirits and well up for tackling the *Alto del Perdón*.

After leaving the village behind, in a few minutes one comes to a fountain at the side of the road, *Fuente de la Teja*.

According to legend the pilgrim in past times could get his gourd filled with water from this fountain at the price of selling his soul to the devil. The fountain was dry as I passed, so I could only suppose too many had agreed to that deal.

The path up from here was steep, and the wind increased as I got higher but I found it manageable. All the talk in the *albergue* the night before was just that, talk. Within an hour I was at the summit admiring the view of the plains on either side, stretching away to the north and south.

At the very top there was a sculpture depicting a group of figures cut from sheet steel that was erected some time ago by the electricity company that owns the wind farm up there. There was an inscription at the base that read: '*Where the way of the wind crosses that of the stars*'. Very appropriate I thought as a strong wind blows constantly up there.

It was time to get off this mountain so I followed the arrows and started to descend down what was a rather loose stone path, with the occasional large boulders to navigate. The path was, however, afforded shelter from the wind by the holm oak and tall box trees on either side, some respite from the constant jarring of the knees was got further down from steps made of timber sleepers.

Eventually I got to the bottom of the descent at the small village of Uterga and I took a break there for another *café con leche*.

From here the path was over a pleasant sandy track through fields and fruit trees, and in another half hour I arrived in Muruzábal. As it was now 2pm, lunch and foot repair time, I adjourned to the only bar in this small hamlet.

From there it was an easy walk of another half hour to arrive at the quaint old town of Obanos, through its ancient gateway that led to the small square with its monumental church and cross. The striking features of this camino town were the ancestral houses with their coat of arms and the metal scallop shells, the symbol of the camino, that are set in the cobbled streets.

I didn't stop but continued on a narrow country road to Puente la Reina, the old medieval town that is one of the most emblematic points on the camino on its passage through Navarra.

When I arrived at the *albergue*, it was to find Graham, Antoinette, Eoin and Sara sitting outside feet up and downing cervezas frías.

I hadn't seen any of them since Pamplona. They must have observed me from afar, because as I eased myself down into a chair to join them, Graham nonchalantly pushes a cold beer across the table to me and said, "James, I've been saving this one for you. I knew you were out there somewhere but would turn up eventually."

Within twenty minutes Taj and Ardith came into view and the celebrations could begin in earnest. Incredibly they were just behind me all day along the way. They had started very early from Pamplona that morning and had made it as far as Zariquiegui just minutes after I had set off from there.

When leaving Puente la Reina at first light the following morning the streets were eerily quiet. For once I was out of the *albergue* early and walking with my *camino amigos* (camino friends).

We set off down the *calle mayor* (main street) passing the Padres Reparadores Monastery and then the church of Santiago with its wonderful pair of Romanesque doors.

Right next to it is the church Iglesia de San Pedro, where legend has it that in ancient times a small bird appeared daily to clean the face of the statue of the virgin here.

Finally, we came to the famous six arch Roman bridge that spans the river Arga. As I walked across it in that early morning light, I was acutely aware of all the pilgrims who had crossed this bridge before me, down through all the years back as far as the tenth century.

From Puente La Reina the countryside is of rolling farmland and vineyards but with few trees and little shelter. We tramped along with the group spreading out, the fast walkers forging ahead and the laggards, including yours truly, bringing up the rear.

After about an hour walking on fairly level ground I came to a long steep stony slope up to the village of Maneru. I found this difficult, but once through the entrance arch to the village, the route wound its way through its narrow streets flanked with quaint dwellings, several of them recently restored.

Beyond the village after passing close to the cemetery, I was able to make out the outline of Cirauqui the next village in the distance.

The winding clay track that linked them proved ideal for walking. The view from here out over this landscape captures the character of this section of the camino so well.

Walking through the small town of Cirauqui one steps back in time. The route wanders along the very old narrow streets, under arches, even through the portico of the town hall and alongside the walls of the two medieval churches there, *San Román* (Saint Raymond) and *Santa Catalina* (Saint Catherine).

On leaving this hilltop town there is a steep descent.

The old Roman bridge at Puente La Reina

When I arrived at the bottom I came to the remains of an old Roman road and a bridge spanning the river Iguste. In Roman times this road linked Astorga with Bordeaux.

As the top layer of sand and gravel that would have made up the surface of this well-travelled road in Roman times has long disappeared, it proved hard walking over the remaining stone foundation of the road, but still a fine example of a Roman roadway and bridge. Perhaps the pilgrim may be forgiven if his imagination jumped back a thousand years as he walked through this history.

From here it's on to the village of Lorca, where halfway along the *calle mayor* I came to a very pretty garden outside a bar just as the faster walkers of my group were preparing to pull out.

However, this unexpected encounter gave them the excuse to extend their leisurely and somewhat liquid lunch to mind me, so to speak. I was reminded of the old adage: 'a snail will eventually get to Jerusalem'.

After a further half hour of this impromptu party it was off again towards Villatuerta and our lodgings for the night in the very pleasant *Albergue Villatuerta*, arriving there in late afternoon.

The next day I was on the road early, walking over nice, easy natural paths. Soon I was approaching the important camino town of Estella. The route into the old town is amazing as it winds its way along the Rúa de los Curtidores, that dates back to what was a very prosperous period of the way of Saint James, with three churches, a monastery and the palace of the kings of Navarra along its length.

One has only to walk past these edifices to appreciate the importance in ancient times of this town to the pilgrims passing through on their way west to Compostela.

Soon I was enjoying my regular coffee stop in the town with several of my walking companions, before hitting the trail again.

All along the camino there are *fuentes* (fountains) where pilgrims can replenish their vital water supplies to sustain them on the journey.

Some are quite elaborate affairs, usually found at the centre of the *plaza mayor* (main square) of the larger villages, while in the smaller *pueblos* (hamlets) there might be just a simple water spout protruding from an old stone wall.

The refreshing cool clear waters are eagerly sought out by the weary and thirsty pilgrim.

So it was that after leaving the town of Estella and enduring a steep climb I came upon one of the most amazing sights along the way, the wine fountain at Irache. *La Fuente del Vino* (the wine fountain), where in keeping with a long tradition, the family of the Bodega del Irache has been dispensing both water and wine free to passing pilgrims for as long as anyone can remember. It goes without saying that I too gracefully accepted their hospitality.

Just further on up the hill is the huge monastery of Irache, now closed and unoccupied, but its sheer size and the church connected to it are evidence of its important past.

To the front of the monastery is a nice, shaded grassy area with stone tables and benches. The whole gang were gathered there when I arrived.

A simple meal was quickly thrown together

from what we were all carrying with us, bread, various cheeses, even tinned spam from Taj's emergency supplies and, of course, the wine of La Irache. 'The craic', as we Irish would say, was mighty with everyone in great form.

Later we continued along pleasant natural pathways through delightful woodlands and fields of lavender together, all of us in good spirits.

By now the walking was getting easier for me as my ligament problem had all but disappeared. I felt fitter and I was walking without any difficulty.

I passed through Azqueta, a hamlet where one of the residents there has become famous on the way for issuing free walking sticks to passing pilgrims.

The route continued along a winding track until I came upon one of the strangest sights I had witnessed so far, a small steep roofed stone building with two open arches to the front and inside steps the width of the entire building leading

La Fuente del Vino at Irache

down to a large cistern at the bottom.

This is *La fuente de los Moros* (the fountain of the moors). Its origins are not known but it dates back to the middle ages. From here I could see the church tower at Villamayor de Monjardín.

The walking continued to be easy until just before the town. A steep hill had to be negotiatedcarefully as the tracks' surface of loose gravel was very slippery.

Villamayor de Monjardín was my destination for the night. Its splendid views over the surrounding countryside were dominated by the conical peak of Monjardín, with the ruins of Castillo de San Estéban forming a distinctive backdrop to the village.

Here I caught up with Graham and Antoinette, who had just arrived ahead of me and had grabbed two of the three last bunks left in the whole place for themselves. They had kindly held the very last one for me.

When the rest of the gang arrived a little later, having taken a detour up to the ruins of Castillo de San Estéban, they had no option but to continue on to Los Arcos. That was another long three hours walking away.

It was three very grim pilgrims who sat down to *la cena* that evening. I remember it as a very quiet meal, even Antoinette who was always full of chat was uncharacteristically silent throughout the whole time.

I think all three of us were grimly affected by this unexpected turn of events at the end of what had been a very enjoyable day on the camino. It had become a very long day indeed for the others.

The three of us were on the road by 6am the next morning and glad to leave this town behind. Within no time the other two had pulled ahead and I continued on at my own pace.

Soon it became apparent that this section was going to be flat and monotonous. I had been warned before I left the *albergue* that the fountain about an hour out along the trail would be the last before Los Arcos.

When I reached it, I stopped briefly to fill up all my water bottles and pressed on. The landscape remained dull with only the odd shed or ruin to be seen along the way. Almost without warning a bench came into view, out here in the middle of nowhere. A nearby sign stated it was where the old church of Yaniz stood, alas now no more.

This was a lonely place, I was alone with not another human to be seen in any direction, so I kept moving and even quickened my pace.

After another hour I reached Los Arcos that was a very important point on the camino in ancient times, but for me it held no appeal as upon enquiring at the bar at the entrance to the village about my *camino amigos* I was informed they had all left over an hour earlier.

So after a very late breakfast of a large slice of *tortilla* accompanied by a small *café solo* (black coffee) reinforced with a large cognac, I hit the road.

Beyond Los Arcos the landscape continued as before, that is to say flat and uninspiring, through the village of Sansol. It then followed an easy descent into the town of Torres del Río. At first sight this town looks like any other a pilgrim will pass through in Navarra as he heads on for the border with La Rioja. Surprisingly, it turned out to be a vibrant place with plenty of services.

It was however the church of *Santo Sepulcro* (Holy Sepulchre) that astounded me. I came to it among the warren of narrow streets that make up the old quarter of this hill town.

It was built in the twelfth century and is octagonal in shape, suggesting it may have been connected to the Knights Templar, but no one seemed to know what its origin was.

It has been in continuous use through the centuries and is still in use to this day. The congregation stands during mass as the nave is without seating.

After leaving Torres del Río, the route follows an earthen track ascending and descending small hills, and wandering through the hamlets of Virgin del Poyo and Viana.

Shortly after the hamlet of Virgin de las Cuevas I came to the sign that announced I was now leaving Navarra behind and crossing into the province of La Rioja.

The sign also mentioned that this spot was a mere 626 kilometres from Santiago de Compostela.

CHAPTER FOUR

Among the vineyards of La Rioja

La Rioja is one of the smallest and yet one of the more diverse of the autonomous regions of Spain. It is sandwiched between the mountains of Navarra and the flat plains of the Meseta of Castilla y León and is justifiably renowned for its wonderful wines and the friendly people who have been welcoming pilgrims since medieval times.

The countryside has changed to open arable farmland since crossing into the province of Rioja and the shade is limited to small isolated stands of pine.

Further on, just before entering the city of Logroño, the way then enters the wine producing region. The entrance to this city is by way of the Puente de Piedra, spanning the river Ebro.

The city itself boasts many attractions for the pilgrim, not least the old town where the shopping street of Portales is located. Strolling from shop to shop through the arches that give the street its name is a very enjoyable way to spend a few hours away from the daily grind of camino.

Also in this area is Calle Laural, crammed full of *tapas* bars and small family restaurants, it is a great pilgrim's nocturnal hangout.

The Cathedral of Santa María la Redonda dominates the skyline of the old town, the city's largest church, it dates from the fifteenth century and is a favourite nesting place for storks high up in its twin towers.

About three kilometres before the city, sitting on a low stone wall at the bottom of a hill, I came upon Taj and his sister Ardith. They are the two pilgrims from Los Angeles of Filipino ancestry, with whom I had crossed paths with along the way.

They both had been suffering from severe blisters almost from the start at St-Jean-Pied-de-Port, often arriving long after everyone else at the hostels at night. It was obvious Ardith was by now in great distress, and although I offered to return with a taxi to collect her she bravely insisted on completing the day's walk.

However, it was to be her last day on the camino, for that evening on doctor's orders she had to concede defeat and make arrangements for what would be a long trip home to Los Angeles for her.

This turn of events, though not unexpected, put a dark cloud over the group. She was very well regarded by all, not least for her quiet and gentle personality and the kind acts of generosity in sharing items with her fellow pilgrims.

When the rest of group headed off next morning, it did so without me. I had been suffering from toothache for some days and needed to have it seen to.

Also I decided that after walking without a break for twelve days I would have to take a rest here in Logroño and booked into a hotel where I was able to wash both myself and my clothes in hot water for a change.

Later I was seen by a dentist who informed me that the tooth needed to be extracted when I returned home. However, he was able to stabilize the problem for the short-term and as I was a *peregrino* (pilgrim) the dentist waived his fee.

One day later, aided by painkillers I was back on the way.

Just before entering the historic camino town of Navarrete I passed the ruins of the St Jean d'Arc monastery that she founded in 1185. Navarrete, is well-known for its pottery, and in the square alongside the church, there are pottery shops selling some very lovely examples of the local art.

Although I was tempted by one fine piece in particular, I demurred and retreated to the bar next door to have a light lunch and to consider the consequences of my proposed investment.

This of course entailed convening a meeting of what I called my 'camino crisis management committee'; a ruthless gang who were tasked with dealing with such matters as the weight of my backpack or, more to the point, efforts of reducing same.

It goes without saying, all pleadings on my part that this expedition could benefit from a little contribution to the arts fell on deaf ears, a stony and uncompromising bunch that lot. I determined there and then that should I make it to Santiago the first thing I would do is sack the lot of them. But for now that lovely piece of Navarrete pottery stayed in Navarrete.

I tramped on thinking maybe I had been walking alone for too long and it was time to catch up with my *camino amigos* again.

Leaving Navarrete, I came to a very large cemetery with an impressive Gothic arch at the entrance. From here the way is along secondary roads with vineyards on both sides and very little traffic.

After a while I fell in with a group of four young Italian lady pilgrims from Naples who had joined the camino in Logroño. I walked with them for a while before pushing on, as they were walking at a very slow pace. "*Vaya con Dios*" (go with God) one said on our parting.

Strangely, this was the first and last time I laid eyes on this group along the way. I wondered whether they ever made it to Compostela.

It is twenty-six kilometres from Logroño to Nájera. I decided that would be my stop for the night, so I marched on through the afternoon heat.

At about 4pm in the afternoon I shuffled into Nájera dead tired and with a troublesome new blister on the outside of my right foot, a match for the one I already had on the other foot. This required the usual surgery with a needle and thread and bottle of Betadine as soon as I booked in to my lodgings for the night.

I later joined some other pilgrims, mostly Spanish, at *la cena*. They were all strangers to me, so I took myself off to bed and was asleep within minutes.

After a good night's sleep, I was on the road by 7am. This was early for me, but I just wanted to get going this morning. So after checking on the new and old blisters, getting them ready for the days walk ahead and with a quick glance in my guide book I was out the door of *albergue* and on my way.

The walk today was on dirt tracks through more vineyards. After two hours walking I entered the town of Santo Domingo de la Calzada, a town steeped in the history of the camino.

Here the descendants of the cock and hen who, according to legend came to life after being roasted, are still living high up in a coop in the transept of the Cathedral of Santo Domingo.

The story goes that sometime in the middle ages a couple and their son on a pilgrimage to Santiago stopped at an inn here for the night.

The innkeeper's young daughter, on having her amorous advances towards the son rejected, secreted a silver goblet in his luggage and then reported to the town authorities that he had stolen it. The result was that he was hanged for his supposed crime. The parents, though devastated, continued on their pilgrimage to Santiago.

On their return journey, when again passing through Santo Domingo de la Calzada, much to their surprise they found their son still hanging from the gallows and incredibly, still alive.

They immediately rushed to the mayor's house where, on finding him about to sit down to his dinner, they declared this to be a miracle. The mayor, not believing them, stated that their son was no more alive than the roasted cock and hen he was about to eat.

The words were hardly out of his mouth when both fowl crowed and jumped off the plate; with that the youth was pardoned. Over the centuries this story has turned into one of the more endearing legends of the camino.

Leaving the town of Santo Domingo de la Calzada behind and crossing over the Puente del Santo and along gravel paths I came to the quiet

Through the vineyards of Rioja

walled village of Grañón, where I had lunch in a small bar on my own. On leaving the village I crossed over a stream and climbed a small hill where a large modern sign announced I was now entering the autonomous region of Castilla y León. All along the way in every village there are churches and monasteries that are steeped in the history of the camino. In a sense this was a walk through the past.

CHAPTER FIVE

A Solitary trek through Burgos

Leaving the wine growing region of La Rioja behind and entering the province of Burgos, the first of the provinces that are part of the autonomous region of Castilla y León, I passed through the small villages of Castildelgado and

Viloria de la Rioja before finally making a stop for the night at Villamayor del Río.

The *albergue* was located in an isolated spot off the main road leading to the village. There were around twenty pilgrims there that night and among them was a character I would put in his mid-sixties. I had seen him on the road before on quite a few occasions.

In fact, every time I met with him I was overtaking him, he walked slowly with a kind of swagger, like a cowboy, probably helped by the two plastic shopping bags he always had with him. He also had a huge backpack.

I would see him up the trail ahead lumbering along and before long I would be abreast of him and after a few words of greeting I would pull ahead, there was never any small talk.

It always puzzled me that even though I would pass him around mid-morning, I never saw him for the rest of the day, but there he would be again the following morning ahead of me.

For some reason the younger pilgrims christened him 'Einstein', so at *la cena* that evening I sat beside him. He told me he was from northern Germany where he lived on the Baltic coast.

It turned out he knew the west of Ireland well, having been there several times as he was a big fan of Irish music. He had, from time to time, acted as a local agent for some of the Irish musicians that toured Germany.

A most knowledgeable and interesting man, he told me he tended to stay in *albergues* in the country or on the outskirts of villages. He would hit the road before sun up and walk at this slow but steady pace for up to eight hours each day. He never did divulge what was in the shopping bags. I was only to meet him once more.

About a week later I overtook him as usual, but this time he indicated for me to stop and we had a chat about this and that. I noticed he had a bandage on his right hand and scratches on his face.

When I enquired what happened to him, he confided he had stumbled and fallen down a bank a few days earlier. I thought he looked a bit shaken. We parted. I was never to see him again.

Although I later enquired of various people who would have been acquainted with him, no one remembers meeting him again.

By lunchtime the next day, after a boring morning's walk on a dusty track alongside the busy N20, I reached Belorado.

Right on cue, there they were, holding court under a big red Coca-Cola umbrella outside the first bar I came to, my two Canadian friends Desiree and Natasha.

They were in the company of a group of pilgrims, none of whom I knew. They seemed to know everyone. I joined them for a cerveza and caught up on the latest camino gossip. They lifted my spirits as they did every time I met them.

The author with the Canadians Desiree and Natasha

Before moving on we agreed to meet up in Burgos which lay two days walking ahead.

The next big test was crossing the Alto de la Pedraja at twelve hundred meters between Belorado and Ages. Right at the summit is the monument to the memory of *Los Caídos* (The Fallen), the fallen of Spain's gruesome civil war of the 1930s.

The monument to El Los Caldos, Spanish Civil War dead

Although I was shattered after the long climb over very rough road, I removed my hat and stood in silence for a while in honour of the fallen, and reflected on the futility of all wars. It was around these mountains that some of the most vicious battles took place, with Irish fighting on both sides. As they say here even the olives were bleeding.

I still had fourteen kilometres to go to San Juan de Ortega to find a bed for the night.

I reached the city of Burgos on Sunday the 7th of June in late afternoon after a twenty-six kilometre walk from San Juan de Ortega. The old quarter with its narrow streets and small *plazas* was alive with people relaxing in the cafes and strolling about in the sunshine.

After booking in for the night in the municipal *albergue* and with no sign of the Canadians, I went off to visit the great cathedral of Burgos, Catedral de Santa María. It is the largest in all of Spain and known for its extravagant magnificence. It is also famous for the tomb of El Cid and his wife Doña Jimena. The sheer scale of this cathedral left me spellbound.

The cathedral together with the surrounding medieval streets in this part of town have been designated a UNESCO World Heritage Site.

Shortly after leaving Burgos behind, the weather started to warm up at last. It continued to get hotter as I tramped along following the yellow arrows marking the way towards Hontanas.

This was a long trek for me, being thirty-two kilometres from Burgos to Hontanas, but I felt up to it. Furthermore, I had been told in Burgos that some of my *camino amigos* were now only about a day ahead of me on the trail.

I was keen to catch up with them after having been walking on my own since way back in Logroño.

The talk in the *albergue* in Burgos the night

before had been all about getting safely through the area that lay ahead, known as the Meseta. An area called *el yunque del diablo* (The Devil's Anvil) by the Spanish for a very good reason.

It entailed days of tramping along through enormous wheat fields stretching as far as the horizon, interspersed every seven to ten kilometres with villages, all now mostly deserted. Walking up to twenty-six kilometres a day with not a human soul to be seen, just the odd hawk in the sky.

So on this section I didn't dally as I passed through the hamlets of Tarjados and Rabé de los Calzados then on to the isolated Fuente de Praotorre. The young trees planted around it gave little shade and the view westwards was of wheat fields stretching to the horizon.

The green wheat crop soaked up the blistering sun and the stalks waved back and forth making a swishing noise in the slight breeze. I was now walking on the highest point of the Meseta and would continue on this eerie plateau for at least another three hours.

Then after what seemed ages, the terrain started to descend sharply until I came to the river Hormazuela. From there it was a hot but easy walk along the river into Hornillos del Camino. This was an important medieval pilgrim stop on the way to Santiago and not much has changed since.

I took a break here and got stuck into a *tortilla* and the usual *cerveza fría* while sitting in the shade outside a bar and taking in the view of the picturesque Plaza de la Iglesia with its *Fuente del Gallo* (fountain of the cock).

Before long I was moving on again. On leaving the town I came to some poplar trees that afforded some shade before the open track again climbs back up onto the Meseta and its world of never ending wheat fields and no shade.

Late in the afternoon I staggered up to the

Albergue el Puntido, in the centre of Hontanas to find my old friends, Taj, Eoin, 'The Scotts' and Roly, lounging about in the shaded courtyard.

They told me Graham and Antoinette were also here and now busy checking out the restaurants of the village as it had been agreed by all that a change from *albergue* food was called for tonight.

Just then, a familiar voice calls out from the balcony above. "James, we have been looking out for you, we heard you were not far behind. How is the tooth? Are you joining us for dinner?"

It's Sara, a pretty and graceful 19-year-old girl from New Mexico of Native American ancestry, her mother belonged to the Kewa Tribe and her father was German. Sara, in my opinion, was by far the best walker in the group and she became a sort of 'Camino secretary' to me along the way, checking out the *albergues* ahead, reserving beds and, of course, finding the best places to eat. I was really drained from today's long march, but in a

Rush hour in Riego de Ambros

strange way I felt energized by meeting up with my friends again after walking mostly alone for the last week or so. "Is the Pope a Catholic or what!" I called back, as I gratefully accepted a *cerveza fría* from Taj.

Ronaldo, or Roly, as he was known to one and all, was nineteen years old, of medium height with Latino features and an engaging smile for everyone he met.

Back home in Miami he was about to start into his last year in college. But for now on the walk he was everyone's favourite; quiet, thoughtful of other pilgrims and always happy.

Any morning, no matter how early it was or how daunting the day's trek appeared, at the first stop for coffee on meeting Roly he never failed to cheer everyone up.

His story, incredible as it may seem, was that he was saved by the US coast guard from certain drowning when he was two years old while trying to get to the USA from Cuba with his family in a small open boat. Where Sara would almost glide along and was always first to get to the day's destination, Roly had only one pace, that of a snail. He also had a very expensive camera.

The extraordinary thing was that more times than not, the two travelled separately and at different paces. Roly usually left the camera behind in the hostel or some bar or cafe along the way, only to be reunited with it after it was carried onwards by a fellow pilgrim.

It was at Burgos that one of life's great characters joined the camino. He was here to walk the rest of the camino with his friend, a furniture store owner from Minnesota, who had been with us from the beginning. He was a consultant in the same industry and came from Chicago.

He was keen to tell all and sundry that he only came along on the camino to ensure his friend returned safely to the civilised world. Both were in their late thirties with the demeanour of the successful American about them. Incredibly they were named Scott and Scot. Collectively they were always referred to as 'The Scotts'.

Now, for two people who were in the same line of work and obviously great friends, whose families even holidayed together, they were like chalk and cheese both in character and personality.

Minnesota Scott, who originally hailed from Canada, was very tall and athletic, he would walk at a rapid pace and had no trouble covering long distances. He was friendly, quietly spoken, thoughtful and considerate with great people skills. I enjoyed passing many a mile walking with him as we discussed the great navigators, explorers, and generally put the world to rights.

Chicago Scot, on the other hand, was of a strong stocky build and not as fit, but with a determined streak. He was one who would not be inclined to suffer fools gladly and was quite opinionated on all things on and off the camino. An entertaining guy to have a glass or two with at the end of the day's walk, tough and uncompromising and very interesting.

For all that, I found him to be generous to a tee, and indeed he more than once along the way gave up the prized bottom bunk to a certain older pilgrim. A true friend indeed.

'The Scotts' had adopted Yuki, a quiet, petite, Japanese girl in her early twenties and there's no other word to describe it but adoption. She was on her way home to Tokyo after a year as an exchange student in America and had stopped off to walk the camino.

As the days wore on, all of us were finding the going progressively more difficult. She was finding it especially so, and carrying an enormous backpack was not helping.

By the time the city of Burgos was left behind it appeared she was almost done in, but in true Japanese tradition giving up was not an option, so she literally staggered on. That was until the cavalry appeared in the form of 'The Scotts'. They came to the rescue by helping to carry her pack which was almost as big as herself, helping her through a very bad patch. She duly recovered to make it all the way. The true camino traditions meeting the old traditions of the East.

I was late, very late, venturing out of the *albergue* in Hontanas the next morning. This could have had something to do with the long gruelling walk yesterday or as some might unkindly put it, this state of affairs I now found myself in had nothing whatsoever to do with walking... I will say no more on the subject.

As it turned out I wasn't the only pilgrim feeling a little delicate that morning. As I left the *albergue* and rounded the corner to the street leading to the exit of the village, I beheld three of the heroes of last night's festivities – wasn't it Taj with Chicago Scot and Eoin.

There they were indulging in refreshments outside the small bar on the other side of the street. The sunny side at that, and at this time of day; not a good sign, as we would be under a hot sun for most of today's walk but indicative of this mornings reduced faculties no doubt.

Naturally I joined them. It would have been

rude not to. After indulging in what one might call the 'hair of the dog', the four of us moved off at last. Normally I would walk faster than Scot or Taj but considerably slower than Eoin, however this was turning out to be, not a normal day, so we walked together along minor concrete roads.

By noon we had passed under the archway at San Anton. After a stop for a late lunch in Castrojeriz we pressed on to *Boadilla del Camino*, our destination for the day. We met up with the rest of the group who had arrived well before us at the quaintly named *En El Camino* (on the road) *Albergue*.

This proved to be one of the nicer hostels along the camino with its lovely garden and small swimming pool, just what was needed at the end of this hard days walking.

29 - 5 - 2014

CHAPTER SIX

The Road is Always West Through Palencia

The Way crosses into the province of Palencia over the eleven-arch Puente de Itero bridge that spans the Río Pisuerga, the boundary between the old kingdoms of Castilla and León.

The land here is used principally for agriculture,

mainly wheat. It is flat, with few trees to offer shade from the relentless sun but with several canals and small rivers to irrigate its rich soil. The buildings in most of the *pueblos* have red earthen walls and cellars built of the same material. Many are caves dug into the hills to store the local wines.

The next day started with an easy walk through the flat Tierra de Campos to the Canal de Castilla. It then followed the tree lined canal bank and over the lock gates before entering the town of Frómista.

It was while dallying here, I took the opportunity to visit the beautiful eleventh century Iglesia de San Martín, considered one of the finest examples of Romanesque church architecture in all of Spain. I wasn't disappointed.

On the 13th of June I reached Carrión de los Condes, the halfway point, with just four hundred kilometres left to walk. This town occupied a very important position on the camino in ancient times.

Once ruled by the Counts of Carrion, old adversaries of El Cid, who, it is said, dispatched

**Carrión de los Condes, the halfway point,
St James is the one on the right**

some of them to an early grave for mistreatment of their daughters.

Today, it has all the services needed by pilgrims, including several hostels and restaurants, but can be very busy and sometimes accommodation for the latecomers can be hard to find.

With this in mind, when I arrived in the main square, I was very glad to see my camino secretary waiting there with the welcome news that she had organized not only the lodgings for the night, but a nice place for us all to dine in later that evening.

From Carrión, the way then continues along dirt tracks and minor roads through wheat, wheat and nothing but wheat, with the *pueblos* of Caldadilla de la Cueza and the small towns of Sahagún and Mansilla de las Mulas the only places of respite from the monotony, dust and stifling heat.

When I arrived in Mansilla de las Mulas late in the afternoon, I found the *albergue* there full and I had no option but to walk on for another six kilometres to Villarente to find a bed, a total for the day of thirty-two kilometres.

On arrival there I just collapsed into my bunk. This proved to be the lowest point for me on the whole camino. When I woke the next morning

I felt I had travelled far enough and should go home after I reached the city of León, twenty-two kilometres further on.

The road is always west, tramping day after day through the Meseta

However, I had not reckoned on my wife Teresa's calm encouragement over several phone calls inspiring me to keep going.

Her logical reasoning was for me to not make a decision I might live to regret, especially as I had decided before starting out that for whatever reason I should not complete my pilgrimage I would not return for another attempt.

Her faith in me renewed my determination to keep going and my belief that I would make it to Santiago.

So on I tramped day after day across the Meseta and in keeping with my regime of a late start each morning, and because of the long distances between villages, I seldom met other pilgrims.

The only company I had along this stretch of the camino was a rather strange individual who always seem to appear about an hour into the day's walk and kept pace with me for the rest of the day.

Although I welcomed the company out there in that wide open and lonely place, my companion turned out to be a very silent type. I never found out who he was or where he came from.

In fact, he never contributed a word to the conversation between us. I noticed, he also had this disconcerting habit of stretching out well ahead of me as the morning advanced.

Around midday it seemed to me he was ten feet tall then as the afternoon progressed he swung around to my right hand side and by late afternoon he had shrunk back to normal size.

The other weird feature was he was dressed quite similarly to myself in every respect, as far as I could make out. But as I said, in spite of every effort to engage him in conversation, by the end of the day's trek I knew as much about him as I did when he first appeared.

He would then disappear as I reached my destination and I never saw him again until the next morning. In the end I just took to calling him 'shadow'. A strange place indeed is the Meseta.

On reaching the city of León I met up with some of my *camino amigos* again. It turned out that most of them were also suffering from both physical and psychological strain, due to the exertions of the trek through the Meseta. So it was collectively decided to take a full day's rest here.

Eoin, Yuki, Scott, Scot, Sara and Taj with the author in front of León Cathedral

León is a beautiful city. Its cathedral is inspiring. Construction started in 1205 and according to the experts it has the purest Gothic style building in Spain. One of its greatest treasures are the magnificent stained glass windows covering a total area of eighteen hundred square metres.

The old town is known as *Barrio Húmedo* (the wet quarter), it is noted for its traditional architecture with its narrow streets and in particular its lively atmosphere that is favoured by the locals for drinks and *tapas*.

The *plaza mayor*, dominated by the old city hall, is without doubt one of the most impressive on the way.

So after a day off the road spent sightseeing and now suitably refreshed, we set out together the following day determined to reach Santiago de Compostela.

Leaving León, the way follows a well-marked track going through the villages of Villar de Mazarife, Villavante and Puente y Hospital de Órbigo.

There I stopped for lunch after crossing over the magnificent medieval bridge spanning the river Órbigo. It is the longest bridge along the way having no fewer than nineteen arches curving along its length.

After a long day of twenty-eight kilometres I reached Astorga, once an important Roman city where the famous tenth Roman Legion was based. The city has been giving shelter, comfort and relieving pilgrims of their money ever since.

The most important feature of the town is the *plaza mayor* with its portico buildings housing numerous bars and cafes and its huge town hall famous for its Maragato clock.

The bishop's residence here is the work of the famous Catalan architect Antoni Gaudí, but I believe it to be one of his lesser works.

On to Ponferrada and Villafranca. These two towns are steeped in camino history and very much associated with the Knights Templar who turned out to be a nasty bunch, by all accounts, until some Pope decided to get rid of the lot.

On the whole, my days on the camino followed

a set pattern. Never wishing to be seen out before the streets were properly aired, I would rise around 7am after most of the pilgrims had already left the hostel.

The author setting out with the streets well aired

Following a wash, usually in cold water, tending to my blisters and packing my bag I would then venture out. I walked alone mostly, usually overtaking Taj, Yuki and some of the other slower walkers before too long, or meeting up with them at the very welcome mid-morning coffee stop at some village or other.

Of course nothing stays the same in life along the camino and this set pattern would be interrupted every Saturday morning by what was to become a sort of institution among my camino amigos and total strangers alike.

It became known as James's Saturday morning soiree. A sort of weekly acknowledgement of our progress along the way, in the form of an informal breakfast gathering every Saturday morning and hosted by me at the first bar we encountered on the walk.

A mark of Irish hospitality towards my fellow pilgrims so to speak. Here I would be found liberally dispensing the liquid half of the early morning sustenance, a *café con leche* fortified with a large cognac for every pilgrim who happened along. Of course under no circumstances would any solid food be entertained on *la quinta* (the bill).

All other mornings, I never tended to linger over the coffee as some would do. I would walk on covering around five kilometres an hour until around midday, when invariably I would arrive at a village just as the faster walkers were about to leave after dallying over a leisurely lunch.

I usually had a light snack, changed my socks and, more times than not, performed some running repairs to my blisters and again the hit the trail.

By now of course it was hot, some days hotter than others, but always hot, especially through the Meseta Alta region.

The pace was dropping as each hour passed, and not only for me. I encountered fellow pilgrims who had left well before me that morning, now moving slowly or taking frequent rests along the way.

Although I was tiring like everyone else on the road I somehow got a second wind so to speak. I even enjoyed the last stretch before arriving at the hostel at the end of the day's walk with my first beer firmly set in my sights.

My *camino amigos* who had arrived earlier would say they could hear James coming long before he arrived by the distinctive click-click noise made by the steel tip at the base of my *bastón* (walking stick).

The protective rubber cap had long since worn away. It became the unspoken announcement of my arrival when I claimed that wonderful first beer of the day.

One of those who would always be there to welcome me as I click-clicked my way into the *albergue* at the end of a day's walking, was Sean:

Walking through a deserted village along the way

a tall, distinguished looking man from Balbriggan in Dublin and a very active member of the Society of the friends of St James.

Sean had several caminos under his belt and also helps staff the Irish desk in the cathedral office in Santiago each summer.

He was walking with his lovely daughter Meadhbh, a great favourite with everyone and his nephew Donal, at 14 years of age the youngest of all the walkers I met.

Sean, Meadhbh, Donal,Taz, Scot, Scott, with the author at the Crucero de San Toribio

But it was his quiet demeanour and the unobtrusive but genuine consideration he had for every one that really stood out. He was considered the father figure of the group and would always be consulted on matters camino. His only vice in life, was that he was an ardent follower of the Dublin Gaelic football team, 'the blue and whites' as he called them.

Some say the camino is not merely a place, but a state of mind where one meets people from all over the world, from all walks of life and of all faiths or none. It was my experience on this pilgrimage to cross paths with some very interesting examples of the same.

Of those I met I would class some as devout, others as religious others still as religiously insane.

I concluded the rest were just the ordinary insane or like myself leaning slightly to the side of eccentricity. Those I got to know were, with few exceptions, wonderful company and I remember them all with fondness.

In among all this microcosm of humanity was a particular oddity, if one can call it that, his name was Stephen. He's a priest from Philadelphia, who specialized in braiding the girls' hair most nights after dinner in the *albergues*.

When I first came across him performing these intricate works of art I thought it a strange pastime for a cleric.

I eventually, of course, had to ask him. "What's with the hair braiding Stephen?" "Ah that" he said, "I grew up in a house full of girls. I was the only boy."

Father, as he was usually referred to, was one of the most unselfish people I have ever met. No day went by without him quietly helping the other pilgrims, whether practically or with encouragement. He was indeed one of the most unassuming but most respected of all the walkers.

However, it turned out that he was a Chaplain in the US Marines just back from a gruelling tour of duty in Afghanistan and was a football fanatic to boot. He was not averse to cutting short the homily at his nightly mass, if it happened to clash with a World Cup match.

Another was Tom, a young guy from Germany, who was in his early thirties, of slim build and fit, a good walker too.

Tom was always there, at every stop along the way, every meal, every discussion – Tom was there. The strange thing was he never spoke very much, certainly not of his own volition. Just always very polite.

In one of my very few conversations with him, he did tell me he grew up in East Germany and trained as a solicitor there, but when the wall came down he moved to Hamburg. Soon afterwards he got disillusioned with law and had since worked in social services there.

Then, one evening, Tom arrived back at the *albergue* after *la cena* with some tree branches and proceeded to fix them into a cross. This work went on late into the night until he was satisfied with the result. The next morning to everyone's astonishment the cross was gone and with it Tom.

I never saw either of them again, but I was to learn later that not only did Tom carry the cross to Santiago but it accompanied him on to the end of the world.

Well, what was considered the end of the world in medieval times – Finisterre. There, overlooking the ocean among the rocks above the lighthouse, he planted the cross.

My last report of Tom's cross came from Scott, who last summer walked the *Camino Portugués* with him. When revisiting Finisterre on completion of their walk, they found the cross still in place, a full twelve months after it was planted there.

The little pueblo of Herrerías is in a lovely, peaceful, leafy, wooded valley, beside the river Valcarce, at the base of the pass that leads up to O'Cebreiro.

It was here that the time had finally come for

Waiting for the laggards. Scott, Scot, Eoin, Sara and Yuki

me to part ways with my *camino amigos*, as by continuing further with the group I would arrive too early for my rendezvous with my daughters in the town of Lugo in three days' time.

The leaving was sad as it always is when you part with good companions knowing you may never see most of them again.

I will always remember *la cena* that night, in the little bar at the Casa Do Ferrero, as the best time I had on the whole adventure. Scot insisted I say a few words to be remembered by.

I obliged him by informing all sitting around the table there that night, that it was my misfortune to have fallen in with a group of *camino amigos* that was populated by dreamers, charmers, rogues and scoundrels – some of whom were exceptionally nice people.

But that I would miss them and would remember them fondly long after this camino was over. With that, in response to my pre-arranged signal the *camarero* (waiter) arrived at the table with the champagne and the party began.

CHAPTER SEVEN

Walking with My Daughters in Galicia

I reached O'Cebreiro on the 24th of June, one month after setting out, and crossed into the last province on the camino, Galicia. The scenery here changed to green countryside with lovely oak and chestnut woods.

The track went through small working farms and the distances between villages were short. Of course with the greenery came the rain which stayed with us on and off for the rest of the way.

At Triacastela I took a diversion to the great Benedictine monastery in Samos. It is in a valley and the first glimpse of it through the trees is very dramatic. It is an incredible place.

The monks living there have been looking after pilgrims since the eleventh century and still do to the present day.

I was accompanied most of the way by Christian, a nephew of 'The Father', who was also keen to see the monastery. I suspected he also probably wanted to have some time to himself on the walk. He was a very laid back guy and a great walking companion.

When I asked him how he ended up doing the camino with his uncle, he said he had found himself at a loose end at home and when Stephen offered to pay his way he jumped at the chance. That's Stephen for you.

First glimpses of the great benedictine monastery of Samos

The next day I had a pleasant walk, mostly following the river to the town of Sarria. This is the starting point for pilgrims intending to walk the last hundred kilometres to the cathedral in Santiago and a very busy place. I got a bed for the night in the *Albergue Los Blasones*, located on the narrow and winding *calle mayor* that wanders uphill through the centre of the old town.

Stephen was already there and at this stage was helping out another priest with an American youth group. He immediately invited me to a mass he was celebrating that evening for the group, in the ancient convent Mosteiro de Madalena at the top of the hill.

When I was walking back down the same hill after the mass he caught up with me. "Did you enjoy the service, James?" I answered in the affirmative and couldn't resist adding, "Well Stephen, now that you have at last got me to go to a mass, I suppose I better return the compliment so to speak. Can I buy you a beer?" He laughed out loud, saying, "I thought you'd never ask".

Later that evening while wandering down the *calle mayor* towards my lodgings, I bumped into, of all people, Roly. He was sitting outside one of the bars there, still attached to that infamous camera. It was introductions all round to a large extended family from the US he had fallen in with some time back along the way.

He introduced me mischievously as Uncle James. We had a great chat. He seemed very happy. The father kindly offered me a beer. While inside ordering it I fell into conversation with the mother and enquired of her if all the youngsters in the party were family. 'Yes James, indeed they are, all five of them', she answers almost resignedly. It was then it dawned on me why my newly acquired nephew looked so happy, they were all girls and as it turned out they were Methodists to boot.

The next day was very special for me as, instead

of heading up the trail I took a bus over to the old medieval walled town of Lugo, a designated UNESCO World Heritage Site. I had arranged to meet up with my two daughters Tracy and Carroll and their friend Yvonne who were flying out to join me there.

The plan was meant to be very simple. On the bus over I reread the email I had received from Carroll the day before, with instructions to just get to Lugo and find the hotel that she had already booked on line. 'You are sure to love it,' the email continued. 'It's very old, very authentic, in a very historical area of the old town. Just book in and relax. We should arrive ourselves in Lugo around 5pm. Can you meet us at the bus terminal?' What could be simpler? I ask myself as I alight from the bus.

I found myself walking under the famous arch at the top of the old town of Lugo at 10am in the morning. At this early hour the population were only beginning to wake up in this part of the world. The narrow streets and squares of this lovely quaint old town were almost empty, just the odd bar or cafe owner sleepily going through the daily routine of opening up, setting out chairs and tables etc.

I ambled into a large square looking out for any sign of the hotel. Just then from nowhere I hear a female voice. *"Está buscando algo?"* (Are you looking for something?) *"Me puede instrucciones pars ir a mi hotel?"* (Can you give me directions to my hotel?) I replied.

Right there and then the plan started to unravel. I turned around and was confronted by an incredible sight. In very good English she called out, "Follow us Irish pilgrim!" And I did. I had no option as she was being dragged along at a healthy pace by the biggest dog I ever saw, a Great Dane but larger and very strong. At the other end of the lead was my very new friend Francisca or Freddy as everyone called her, or so she informed me. She was no more than three feet tall, a dwarf. I was never to get the hound's name as we were off and running – so to speak.

The Great Dane led the way, pulling Freddy along, with the backpack laden pilgrim in their wake, trying to keep up. We were going in a downhill direction; the narrow streets were turning into narrow lanes.

The lovely landscaped squares now left far behind and it was apparent to me we were heading down through a rather shabby rundown area, all the time Freddy rattling away about Ireland.

She could name cities, towns and villages and even some well-known bars, up and down the country. Eventually even the Great Dane had to very briefly stop to catch his breath. Although I was panting I was able to ask her how she knew so much about my country. "Couldn't you tell?" she asked. "I went there many times with a circus. I was an acrobat on the horses but I am now retired." And with this disclosure we were off again, still on a downward slope.

I was now beginning to get a little worried and started to think maybe I shouldn't be down in this kind of area at all. Surely no self-respecting hotel could be found down here.

Just then my level of anxiety shot up a notch, for I began to take notice of some ladies standing in doorways, no, not standing rather leaning against door posts as we shot past.

Leather boots up to their thighs, tight skirts that might be more correctly described as belts, blouses open down to the navel and the faces caked with makeup and with red, very bright red, lips. A mad panic flashed through my mind, that was now in turmoil. I could be murdered here.

Just then we turned a corner into a small but very charming little square, with a lovely scent wafting downwards from the Bougainville draped wrought iron lace balconies. The hotel at last is before me. Beyond it was an arch in the town wall, through which a taxi had just driven and was discharging guests at the hotel door.

"I hope you will enjoy your stay in Lugo. We like to help pilgrims here," Freddy said, very matter of fact. The Great Dane just stood there slobbering.

I presented myself, more dishevelled than usual and in a bog of sweat at reception. They were expecting me and my room was ready. It was everything my daughter said it was. Antiques everywhere.

When I was shown to my room I dropped my backpack on the floor and threw myself down onto the lovely, huge big antique bed, testing its softness. In less than a minute I was in a deep sleep.

I had this mad dream. My daughters were on their way out to join me. They bought a newspaper at the airport. The headlines screamed: Irish Pilgrim Murdered by Whores ably assisted by a Dwarf and a Great Dane. The atrocity is reported to have happened in broad daylight, at approximately ten fifteen in the morning. When I woke with a start it was late afternoon. I had been out cold for five hours.

At the appointed time, I was standing there in the bus terminus when the girls bus pulled in. Yvonne who was first to alight turned to the others and announced, "Your father doesn't look anything like a pilgrim to me. He's dressed more like a tourist".

She wasn't to know I had spent the last hour ironing my going ashore uniform for their arrival. I was, of course, delighted to see them. After they checked into the hotel we went for a meal in that lovely square where the mornings high drama had begun.

Sitting there I got to wondering was the whole

thing a dream after all. Maybe the excessive heat of the last few days was getting to me. Then Carroll casually said, "It's a really lovely hotel isn't it? And so traditional. Of course it is in a red light district. We didn't want to tell you that in the email. I hope you don't mind. Do you?" What could I say?

The next day we started together on the last hundred kilometres to Santiago.

With my daughter Tracy at the 100 kilometre marker

It was a very pleasant experience for me to be able to walk the rest of the journey in their company after journeying so far on my own.

Carroll is a teacher in her mid-forties, a good organizer and is very easy going, someone who takes life as it comes. She is slightly built but fit and having seriously prepared for the camino, had little or no trouble completing the distances each day.

Her older sister Tracy on the other hand is the proprietor of the well-known and busy Lemon Leaf cafe in Kinsale. As could be expected, as a business owner she had less time to prepare so was not as fit and found the going tough in places but coped well nevertheless.

Their friend Yvonne, a cardiac consultant in Galway was an experienced walker having already trekked at high altitude in South America. It was something of a boost to my ego to be able to introduce her to my fellow pilgrims as my personal consultant.

Though in reality she was more interested in tending to her own blisters and relaxing with a few vinos (glasses of wine) each evening than listening to an old pilgrims' complaints, real or imagined. The most I ever managed in the way of a free consultation was her standard "You're doing fine. Have another *vaso*" (glass).

Leaving Sarria, the first day was a difficult hike of twenty-four kilometres starting along natural paths and shaded tree lined country roads passing through many small hamlets.

Later in the day it meandered along rough tracks and over several streams. Eventually our path crossed the bridge over the river Mino, and finally before us was the famous but daunting flight of one hundred steps up to the town of Portomarín and to *O'Mirador Albergue*, our lodgings for the night, with its fine dining area and lovely views over the valley and the river below.

The church here, the austere looking Romanesque church of San Juan, otherwise known as San Nicolás, was moved from its original position lower down the hillside and rebuilt stone by stone in its present location before the valley was flooded when a dam was built in 1962.

The next morning, we were on the road by 7:30am in a light rain. The route climbed for an hour through woodland to the main road and after walking for over another hour in deteriorating weather we reached the village of Ventas de Narón, where we were very glad to seek shelter at the first cafe we came to.

Still raining, we started the climb up over the Sierra Ligonde then descended to Portos. Then it was a gentle climb around the lower side of Alto Rosario to continue down to our destination for the day at Palas De Rei.

Tired and wet we were very glad to settle in for the night in the welcoming *Buen Camino*

Albergue there.

The following morning, although overcast, the weather was an improvement on the previous day. We set off in good spirits.

The Way was by now getting very crowded with several large groups walking together. Most were on organized tours and had their backpacks ferried ahead each day by van. In fact, it was not unknown that some even accompanied their bags in the van, to mind them – so to speak.

Our destination for the day was Ribadiso, twenty-six kilometres away through the *pueblos* of Casanova and O Coto. We followed a lovely track through oak woods and across the old medieval Magdalena bridge over the Río Seco into the village of Disicabo.

The Way continued through Gándarra and on to Furelos. From there the climb to Melide is through its modern suburbs.

Tracy and Yvonne crossing over a stream in Galicia

Here, of course, we had to try the traditional regional specialty of *pulpo* (octopus), served in all the cafes in the old quarter.

Then on towards Ribadiso following a path that meanders through a forest of oak and chestnut, then eucalyptus and pine before passing through the villages of Boente and Castañeda. Eventually we reached our destination of Ribadiso late in the afternoon.

From Ribadiso the next morning we followed paths under the shade of large eucalyptus trees. Further on there was a steep climb up the Alto de Santa Irene before we came to O Pedrouzo after a walk of twenty-two kilometres. This is the last town before Santiago and would be our last night on the camino.

We encountered difficulty finding an *albergue* here that was not full, until eventually we found lodgings in a very modern establishment down near the river. The two Canadian girls I had been crossing paths with all along the way were there and they joined us for dinner.

The next day was the last on the camino, with a mere seventeen kilometres left to walk. We started out at 7am and after an hour's uphill walk that took us through a lovely oak wood, we came across a memorial tablet set in a stone wall at the side of the track.

It was in memory of a pilgrim who had died at this spot. He was sixty-nine years old and was so close to completing his camino.

Along the way one comes across such memorials put up by family and friends of pilgrims who have died from natural causes or were killed in accidents while undertaking this journey. Though all are sad to behold, this last one was particularly so and affected us all.

After walking all morning, we came to a place that every pilgrim that set out on the Way of St James has dreamed about reaching.

Memorial to pilgrim

It is known as *Monte del Gozo* (The Hill of Joy). A hill from where one can glimpse the twin towers of Santiago Cathedral through the trees, a mere four and a half kilometres away. In ancient times, the pilgrims would spend their last night here, burning their old walking rags, then washing themselves and preparing for their entrance to the city the following day.

Standing there on top of that hill was a great moment of achievement for me.

CHAPTER EIGHT

The End of the Journey in Santiago De Compostela

After getting our last *sello* stamped in our *Credencial del Peregrino* in the tiny chapel of San Marcos located on top of Monte del Gozo, we started the long descent down the hill known as Rúa do Peregrino.

We walked down a flight of steps at the far end, then over a rail line. We had arrived in the modern suburbs of the city of Santiago Compostela.

After what seemed like a lifetime walking through these suburbs, at last we walked under the famous *Porta do Camino* (The Gate of the Way) at the entrance to the old quarter and on into the magnificent Prazo Obradoiro to arrive at the zero kilometre stone marker.

Finally standing at the base of the steps leading up to the famous Portico de Gloria, the main entrance to the Cathedral of Santiago. It was the end of the journey at last.

I had completed my camino. I was now entitled to claim a *Compostela* that is given to every pilgrim who can prove he or she has completed the pilgrimage by having his or her *Credencial del Peregrino* (pilgrim passport) stamped in every *albergue* stayed in along the way.

I had walked eight hundred and sixteen

kilometres carrying my backpack every step of the way from St-Jean-Pied-de-Port in France, over the Pyrenees and across the north of Spain to the Shrine of Saint James in Santiago De Compostela, in a total of forty-three days.

It was 2pm in the afternoon on the 1st of July 2014. I was seventy years old. I had completed my camino. In my heart I felt an overwhelming sense of humility even though I was physically shattered.

Arriving at the Cathedral in Santiago with Tracy, Carroll and Yvonne

The next morning after breakfast we strolled over to the Pilgrim Office and joined the queue of pilgrims, that even at this early hour had formed outside.

They were all patiently waiting to have their passports checked and would hopefully qualify to receive a *Compostela*. After twenty minutes or so I was finally at the head of the queue and it was my turn. Inspecting my *Credencial del Peregrino* and checking through the long list of sello I had acquired, each one representing an *albergue* I had stayed in along the camino.

"You have walked unaided all the way from St Jean-Pied-de-Port carrying your pack, and that will be announced from the altar at today's pilgrim mass", the official said as he writes Don James Keoghan on my *Compostela* and then stamps it. He shakes my hand as he presents me with it, saying *"Bienvenido a Santiago, Peregrino Irlandés."*

Afterwards, the four of us go over to the cathedral for the noon pilgrim mass. We enter through the south door off the *Plaza Platerias* (the silversmiths square).

We are thirty minutes early and get seats in the second row and spend the time waiting for the mass to start observing the arrival of the washed and unwashed, yesterday's arrivals and those who have just arrived respectively.

On the stroke of noon, the great doors of the cathedral are closed, the place is now packed to the rafters. The organ blasts as the long procession of priests make its way up the main aisle to the altar. One of them then welcomes us all and proceeds to read out a long list of greetings to several pilgrims, among them my own.

The mass is in Spanish and it is probably the most exuberant I have ever witnessed, at the end there is the spectacle of the *botafumeiro* (incense burner) flying through the air.

Spectacle of botafumeiro flying through the air

This massive silver incense burner is swung from one side of the transcript to the other by eight deacons clad in burgundy habits. It reaches almost up to the roof before swishing down just above the heads of the congregation below trailing a cloud of incense behind it.

Its origins are said to go back to some bishop in medieval times who took exception to the smell pervading from some of the poor and destitute pilgrims, who after months on the camino arrived there with nothing more the rags they wore.

Later in the evening I was making my way across the Plaza de Obradoiro to meet my daughters at the Hostal de los Reyes Católicos when I heard, "James! James, it's me, Yuki!"

I could not believe it. There she was, heading for the train station to start her long journey back home to Tokyo, her prized *Compostela* in its protective tube sticking out of her backpack.

Now Yuki was so quiet and timid on the walk that the only response I ever got from her was a smile when I occasionally asked her how she was coping.

I was of course delighted to be able to catch up on news of our walking companions, who by now had all left Santiago and were on their own way home, she being the last.

She just had time to join us for a hurried coffee

and Santiago tart on the hotel terrace before heading off.

As I watched her hurrying through the crowds in the square towards the train station I felt a lump in my throat, for it struck me that I would, in all probability, never see her or most of my other *camino amigos* again.

I looked once more but she had disappeared. This was a defining moment for me, the end of my camino.

Carroll and Yvonne relaxing at Compostela

After two very enjoyable days in Santiago the girls returned home and I flew to Alicante and took a bus down to the small town of Vera in Andalucía.

There I was collected by my good friend Jerry for the short drive over to the old fishing village of Villaricos, where I intended to spend a week before returning home to Ireland.

I have been going to Villaricos for over ten years. It is particularly lovely at that time of the year, the ideal place to recuperate after the exertions of the camino.

So, two days after my arrival, I was surprised and delighted to receive an email from my old walking buddy Taj.

It turned out that he hadn't yet left Spain but instead had lingered in Madrid for a few days seeing the sights before deciding to come south to Granada to visit the famous Alhambra.

I immediately replied and invited him to join me for a few days on the coast in Villaricos.

When he alighted from the bus the next morning at the bus station in Vera, still loaded down with that enormous backpack with various bits and pieces of hiking equipment hanging off the outside, he looked worn out. After having been on the road for over five weeks at this stage, like myself, he was in dire need of some rest.

It was great to see him again and the next few days were spent, apart from a daily dipping of our slowly healing feet in the Mediterranean, just chilling out around the village. Taj has what could be called a natural flair for chilling out and went about it in an all embracing manner.

Serious time had to be devoted to long lunches, mostly liquid, reminiscing on the adventures we had together on the camino, the people we met along the way and the places we passed through. In turn I introduced him to a phenomenon of this village known as the '*Three O'Clock Club*', of which I have the honour of being an esteemed member.

This club has no rules, no subscription, no president, not even a standing committee. Occasionally a semblance of order might be kept by my good friend Jerry, but that is usually completely ineffective. Most afternoons it can be found in session down in the village square at the Plaza Bar.

The genial owner Mark, ably assisted by his two vivacious barmaids Mickela and Kizi, ensures that no member dies of thirst. On occasion it might go on tour, so to speak, and convene outside an establishment known to one and all as Peppy's bar, located at the opposite end of the village.

The problem with this ad hoc arrangement is one never knows from one day to the next what direction to take when leaving the casa. The members are mostly expats living in the village, with a few Spanish characters thrown in.

Nothing is off limits, discussions could range from high finance to low morals in high places and everything in between.

From time to time, as the session wears on, it is not unknown for a sing-song to develop. A most civilised way to master the art of chilling out.

But all too soon it was back to the bus station in Vera to see Taj off to start his long journey home to Los Angeles. "*Buen camino amigo*", was his parting salutation as he boarded the bus. "*Y tú también amigo*", I responded as I watched it pulling away. He waved once then was gone.

Next morning it was my turn to board the bus for Alicante. From there I took a direct flight to Cork, arriving back at my home in Currahoo by late afternoon. I was glad to be back among family and friends, it seemed like I had been gone a very long time.

Before I turned the key in the door I stood for a moment to take in the familiar view down the creek to the river, now at high tide.

Looking across to the opposite bank, my gaze wandering further north towards Ardmartin Hill, and the site of the battle where this story began all those years ago.

It seemed so peaceful now, the summer evening air still with a light heat haze over the countryside. The only noise to be heard was the muted sound of a tractor working somewhere in the distance. Life was just going on.

I had this strange feeling standing there taking it all in but also a sense of achievement. I had fulfilled my pilgrimage to the Shrine of Saint James in Santiago de Compostela to honour the memory of my ancestors. I had completed my camino.

I turned the key, the house was just as I left it. Just then the phone rang and the spell was broken.

It was my friend Brian. "So you're home at last. You must be knackered from all the walking. I am getting the boat ready for a sail with some of the lads. The tide is about to ebb. Come and tell us all about it".

Yes, indeed, life just goes on.

Aftermath of the battle of Kinsale and the Siege of Dunboy

The Battle of Kinsale took place on Christmas Eve 1601. After the defeat of the Irish army, the Spanish garrison under the command of Don Juan del Águila held out for a further week before agreeing to honourable terms of surrender and were allowed return to Spain. The Castles of Baltimore, Castlehaven and Dunboy which were garrisoned by Spaniards were also to be handed over to the English.

Of the Irish leaders, Hugh O'Neill, The Earl of Tyrone, had returned to Ulster. Red Hugh O'Donnell, The Earl of Tyrconnell, had left for Spain. The remaining Gaelic chieftain in the south, Donal O'Sullivan Beare, had returned west to his homeland on the Beara Peninsula. There he regained possession of Dunboy, his main castle, that lies at the western entrance to Bantry Bay.

O'Sullivan Beare appointed Captain Ristéard Mac Eochagáin as commander of Dunboy Castle in his absence and preparations were make for the siege that was certain to come. Mac Eochagáin's whole garrison numbered 143 men. They also had ten cannons left by the evacuating Spanish and O'Sullivan Beare hoped that the Irish soldiers at Dunboy would hold out until O'Donnell returned from Spain with help.

Sir George Carew the Lord Deputy of Munster, on the orders of Queen Elizabeth, set out from Cork City with 3,000 men and was joined in Bantry by Sir Charles Wilmot with 1,000 more. The whole army then moved to Bare Island by sea in the first days of June. Three English warships, The Merlin, The Trinitie and The Hoy, also arrived and were at Carew's disposal.

Faced across the narrow western entrance to Bantry Bay by this powerful array of armament and overwhelming force, the Dunboy garrison prepared for the attack that began on the 6th day of June. For eleven days the bombardment continued from land and sea until on the 17th of June. With the castle now in ruins, Carew ordered a general assault. The garrison resisted the attack from this overwhelming force for a full day with the crews of the ten small cannons fighting with outstanding heroism throughout the siege.

Again and again volunteers came forward to fill the positions of their comrades who lay dead or dying beside the guns. Among them was Mac Eochagáin's own son Brian. When the castle was finally captured not a single cannon remained intact. These gun crews had severely punished the attacking forces and had succeeded in sinking two of the three war ships.

By nightfall the remaining defenders were finally driven back into the cellars where the fight continued hand to hand. Mac Eochagáin, who was lying on the floor mortally wounded, is reputed to have snatched a lighted torch and exerting all his remaining strength staggered towards some barrels of gun powder but was cut down before he could reach them.

There was to be no quarter given to the fifty-eight defenders who were taken prisoner, most of them badly wounded

All were hanged by Carew, the rank and file on the ruins of Dunboy and the remaining officers in the nearby town of Castletownbere. The last to die was the chaplain Rev. Dombnach O'Coilean (Collins) a Jesuit, in his home town of Youghal.

Postscript

I first set foot in Spain, in the port of Bilbao in May 1960, a very young merchant seaman on board the cargo ship Palayo out of London and thus began my long affection for Spain.

We were to spend the summer trading along the Spanish coast, as far south as Casablanca in Morocco.

On that very beautiful Galician early summers evening, a passenger ferry docked at the quay astern of us. People were disembarking on foot and carrying backpacks, I asked one of the Spanish stevedores who they were. *"Son peregrinos que van a Santiago, Señor"* came the curt reply.

How was I to know then that some fifty-four years later I too would become one of those pilgrims. The first Keoghan or Mac Eochagáin, my family name in Irish, to make the pilgrimage to the shrine of Saint James on foot. I would not however have been the first of my family to do so but for a historical decision made four hundred years ago at the great council of war held at Innishannon on the Bandon river to where the defeated Irish army had retreated after the Battle of Kinsale.

The momentous decisions made that fateful December night in 1601 changed the course of Irish history and marked the end of Gaelic rule forever.

Essentially it was decided that the Great O'Neill, the Earl of Tyrone, would return to Ulster to secure his lands there.

Red Hugh O'Donnell, the Earl of Tyrconnell was to leave immediatcly for Spain to seek further help and a force of 400 Irish and Spanish troops under the command of Ristéard Mac Eochagáin, the senior gallowglass captain to the Earl of Tyrconnell, was to go west with the O'Driscoll and the O'Sullivan Beare clans in a desperate attempt to help defend their territories there.

On Sunday the 27th of December, just three days after the battle, when the ship carrying the Earl of Tyrconnell sailed from Castlehaven for Spain my ancestor was not among his entourage on board.

After a stormy passage lasting seven days they made land at Luarca on the coast of Asturias from where they continued to the port of La Coruna.

The Earl and his party then travelled overland to Santiago de Compostela where they worshiped at the Shrine of Saint James before journeying on to Vallodolid for an audience with King Philip III of Spain to seek the help that was never to come.

The rest as they say, is history.

I dedicate my Pilgrimage to the Shrine of St James to the memory of my ancestors Captain Ristéard Mac Eochagáin and his son Brian, who but for a quirk of history would have reached Santiago de Compostela 412 years before me, instead they died at the Siege of Dunboy in September 1602.

James Keoghan

Kinsale

Christmas 2015

Credencial del Peregrino

Hardness of heart and selfishness.

These are your stones;

Leave them at Santiago

(Confraternity of St James-English)

Lightning Source UK Ltd.
Milton Keynes UK
UKOW07f1229170416

272351UK00005B/17/P